Introduction to
Project Planning

APM SIG GUIDES SERIES

Directing Change: A Guide to Governance of Project Management
ISBN: 978-1-903494-15-8

Co-Directing Change: A Guide to the Governance of Multi-Owned Projects
ISBN: 978-1-903494-94-3

Models to Improve the Management of Projects
ISBN: 978-1-903494-80-6

APM Introduction to Programme Management
ISBN: 978-1-903494-63-9

Interfacing Risk and Earned Value Management
ISBN: 978-1-903494-24-0

Prioritising Project Risks
ISBN: 978-1-903494-27-1

Earned Value Management
ISBN: 978-1-903494-26-4

Introduction to Project Planning

APM Planning Specific Interest Group

Association for Project Management

Association for Project Management
Ibis House, Regent Park
Summerleys Road, Princes Risborough
Buckinghamshire
HP27 9LE

British Library Cataloguing in Publication Data is available
ISBN 10: 1-903494-28-1
ISBN 13: 978-1-903494-28-8

Cover design by Mark Design
Typeset by RefineCatch Limited, Bungay, Suffolk
Copy editor: Merle Read
Publishing Manager: Ingmar Folkmans

Contents

Contents

List of figures

Foreword

When you are about to start a project, organise an event or launch a new product, good planning is vital. Good planning is the basis of all good projects. Planning, like many important processes, looks simple. But it isn't. The evidence to prove that is all around us in the projects that for one reason or another have failed. There are just as many good projects, however, and many superb examples of first-class planning.

The point of this publication is to raise the profile of planning and put it in its rightful place at the forefront of project management. Each generation has its leading planners and success stories. It is right that each generation of planners revisits the ideas underpinning planning to see if there is something new, or something worth restating.

The publication of this APM SIG Guide heralds the rebirth of the APM Planning SIG. We hope its light will burn brightly and encourage those of us who are already planners, those who aspire to be good planners and those of us who work with planners. In a sustainable way, of course.

The APM is an organisation serving its membership and driven by individuals. You might be one yourself. You might make a contribution like this one, someday. Stay in touch.

Mike Nichols,
Chairman of the Association for Project Management

Acknowledgements

This *Introduction to Project Planning* has been prepared by the current committee of the APM Planning Specific Interest Group (SIG), with contributions from Ken Sheard (SIG chairman), Neil Curtis (lead author), Andrew Chillingsworth, Ian Granville, Allan Jones, Pete Mill, Mike Prescott and Paul Waskett. It summarises the views of the Planning SIG committee.

The APM *Introduction to Project Planning* builds on work performed by the original Planning SIG committee, chaired by Tony Ciorra, and, in alphabetical order: Mike Harvey, Phil Lewey, Colin Payne and Ken Sheard.

Information about the APM Planning SIG can be found in Appendix C.

1

Introduction

The *APM Body of Knowledge* (*APM BoK*) defines project management as 'the process by which projects are defined, planned, monitored, controlled and delivered so that agreed benefits are realised.' The APM *BoK* defines planning as 'the process of identifying the means, resources and actions necessary to accomplish an objective.'

The APM Planning SIG (see Appendix C) has a particular interest in project planning and believes that:

- Good project planning is critical to project success.
- Planning should therefore be at the heart of successful project management.
- Planning overlaps with and is key to integrating many individual project management disciplines (Figure 1.1).

Figure 1.1 *Planning is at the heart of project management*

1

Introduction to Project Planning

The Planning SIG also believes that:

- The meaning of project planning is misunderstood by many in the project management community.
- The value of effective planning is only occasionally recognised.
- Education and training in planning practice is limited and often poor.
- Good planning practice is often neglected.
- The discipline of planning is undervalued.

As a result of these factors, the central contribution of good planning to project management is not fully appreciated, and it often does not make its maximum contribution to project success. The purpose of this APM *Introduction to Project Planning* is therefore to raise awareness of project APM planning, and to stimulate debate in the project management community in general and in the planning community in particular. It addresses five key questions:

- What is project planning?
- Why plan?
- When to plan
- Who plans?
- How to plan.

It also ventures to define the characteristics of good planning. It does not include a detailed treatment of planning tools and techniques: the Planning SIG intends to address these in future publications.

2

What is project planning?

The unique, transient nature of a project means that a strategy and a plan for its execution must be developed. A project with a good strategy and that is properly planned has a far greater chance of success than a poorly planned project. Planning develops the strategy, and enables the project manager and the project sponsor to determine how the project can achieve its objectives and deliver the required benefits. Hence planning is a key element of project management.

Planning is the process of identifying the means, resources and actions necessary to accomplish the project's objectives. It achieves this by drawing on the expertise and knowledge of an organisation (including the lessons that it has learned from previous projects), and on external parties if appropriate, in order to:

- understand the need, problem or opportunity that the project will address and the benefits that it will deliver;
- determine the business case for, and the success criteria/objectives of, the proposed project;
- define what has to be accomplished and delivered, typically stated in terms of scope, time, cost and quality;
- develop a plan to achieve the deliverables.

Planning commences during the project's concept phase and continues through definition and into implementation. It starts with the project strategy and an initial concept of the need and objectives of the project. It evaluates options and identifies the optimum. Its outputs inform and increase the maturity of the project strategy and objectives through iteration, and provide information for the business case. It delivers much of the information that enables the organisation, through gate reviews (at the end of life-cycle phases or at other key points in the project), to determine whether the project is viable and should be allowed to continue.

Introduction to Project Planning

Planning contributes to the preparation of, and is recorded by, the project management plan (or other formal documentation, which may vary from organisation to organisation) – see Figure 2.1. The PMP (or its equivalent) documents the outcome of the planning process and subsequently provides a reference document for managing the project. The

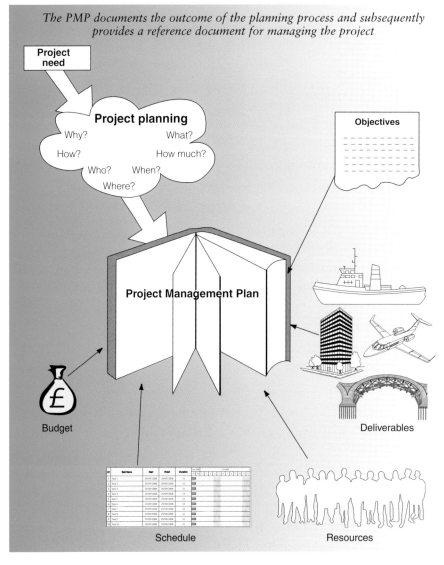

Figure 2.1 *Planning is recorded in the project management plan*

PMP is owned by the project manager and confirms agreements between the project manager, the sponsor and other stakeholders. It is approved by the sponsor, representing the organisation, and by the project manager, representing the project team. Sharing the PMP with stakeholders is important in establishing common agreement of the project, especially as the stakeholders' expectations of the project may have changed during the planning process. Although the project manager owns the PMP, it should be developed with the project team during planning: this removes ambiguity, develops commitment and assists in effective handover of the project from planning to execution.

The PMP documents how the project will be managed in terms of the following questions: why, what, how (and how much), who, when and where.

- 'Why' is a statement of the change to be delivered by the project, which includes a definition of the need, problem or opportunity being addressed and the benefits to be delivered. This is frequently developed in the business case.
- 'What' describes the objectives, the scope, the deliverables and their acceptance criteria. It also describes the success criteria for the project and the key performance indications that will be used to monitor its progress. The 'what' needs to take into account the project's constraints, assumptions and dependencies.
- 'How' defines the strategy for management and execution of the project, its handover, the processes, resources (people, facilities, equipment, tools and techniques) to be used and the monitoring, control and reporting arrangements.
- 'How much' defines the project's cost and budget, the breakdown of the budget and the cost monitoring process.
- 'Who' includes a description of key project roles and responsibilities and of the resources that will be required during execution.
- 'When' defines the project's sequence of activities and timescales, including milestones and any phases/stages.
- 'Where' defines the geographical locations where the work will be performed, which impacts on resources, timescales and costs.

The PMP also describes the policies and plans for managing changes, communication, configuration, governance, health, safety and environment matters, acquisition/procurement, quality and risk.

The PMP is progressively developed during planning and is subsequently managed as a live, configuration-controlled document. Once agreed, the PMP provides a baseline description of how the project will be executed, which is then periodically reviewed and updated through change control. This is especially important where a contractual relationship exists between the project team and client.

It follows that planning must contribute to or determine the why, what, how, how much, who, when and where of the proposed project. Planning therefore has to generate a wide range of outputs, including:

- technical solutions (in conjunction with the product design process);
- scope of supply/deliverables and their acceptance criteria;
- implementation strategies, such as the acquisition/procurement strategy;
- scope of work, usually defined by a work breakdown structure (WBS);
- definition of the processes and resources to be used;
- project organisation, often defined by an organisation breakdown structure (OBS);
- responsibilities for the work, which may be defined by a responsibility assignment matrix (RAM);
- logical sequence for the activities in the work breakdown structure, their interdependencies and durations, and the project's critical path;
- cost estimate, related to the work breakdown structure and providing a basis for allocation of budgets and for earned value management;
- definition of constraints, assumptions, dependencies and risks, including definition of risk responses and contingency provisions.

It is evident that planning is non-trivial: is an intellectual process which should harness the full knowledge, experience and potential of the organisation, with all the lessons it has learned, measurements it has made and new ideas it can muster. It calls on various disciplines including scope management, scheduling, resource management, risk management, cost estimating and budgeting, and earned value management. It is *not* just about planning tools or software, although they have their role in helping

to develop and document the plan. Neither is planning merely the
province of specialist planners, although planners are likely to be involved
in planning all but the most simple projects – it must be owned and driven
by the project manager with involvement of the project team, the sponsor
and other stakeholders.

Having so much leverage on the likelihood of successful project execution, planning has great potential to add value to the management of
projects. The extent of planning should be appropriate to the size and
complexity of the project, but planning should never be omitted.

3

Why plan?

3.1 Reasons to plan

The fundamental reason to plan is to maximise the chances of project success. There are numerous additional reasons:

1. *To light the way forward.* Planning includes the evaluation of options for project implementation. Evaluation of options ensures that the best strategy for the project is selected and can be committed to by all key stakeholders, since all can see which option can best deliver the project's objectives. Organisations in some sectors formalise the evaluation of options in value engineering, in which options are related to project objectives based on what the client (or sponsor) considers to be important.

2. *To obtain commitment.* Projects require commitment from everyone concerned. One of the best ways to ensure commitment is to build the plan with the inputs of all concerned, thus gaining buy-in from everyone working on the project.

3. *To facilitate effective communication.* Communication is important to effective project management and in all but the most trivial projects requires specific management. The PMP defines the objectives of the project and how it will be implemented: on larger or more complex projects, it should define specifically how project communications will be managed. Elements of the plan communicate particular information: for example the schedule communicates when activities must occur, so that resource availability can be managed.

4. *To provide the basis for effective project monitoring and control, and a baseline against which progress can be measured.* In particular, the schedule and the budget define the baseline against which progress is monitored so that any variances can be identified and corrective actions taken.

5. *To prepare for the unexpected.* As with many things in life, all projects can be subject to the unexpected. Planning provides the baseline

8

against which variances can be identified and corrected. Planning should also include considerations of uncertainty and risk. Statistical methods (e.g. Monte Carlo simulation) enable organisations to model the potential range of project outcomes, particularly with regard to schedule and cost. Identification of risks during planning reduces the number of 'unknown unknowns' and enables contingency plans and budgets to be established should adverse events occur.

6. *To respond to compulsory requirements.* Previously, organisations might only have had to produce formal accounts, but compulsory requirements may now extend into the project management arena in general and planning in particular – via, for example, ISO 9001 and corporate governance requirements, a project-based organisation must meet relevant standards.

7. *For use as a basis for arbitration.* Some project-based organisations have learned an expensive lesson through the courts that it pays to have proper plans, to update them regularly and to be in control of scope change. These organisations pay out huge legal fees, on top of which are the time and cost of preparing claims: this is not a cheap option for any organisation, and it is generally much more cost-effective to plan properly.

3.2 Relevance to different types of organisation

Planning, and the plans it produces, is important to numerous types of organisation, but its relevance varies according to type:

1. *The client organisation.* A client organisation requires the deliverables of the project, needs the benefits that the project is intended to deliver and pays for the project, but chooses not to implement the project itself – it selects a contracting organisation for that purpose. Client organisations include the high-street bank which requires new account management software, the train-operating company which requires a new signalling system and the ministry of defence which requires a new air defence system for its nation's air force.

The client organisation must build a business case for the deliverables of the project, undertaking sufficient of its own planning to be able to define its needs in terms of scope, time and cost. The planning undertaken should be sufficient to ensure that the client is an 'informed customer', able satisfactorily to compete and contract for the project, and to judge the merits and feasibility of proposals and plans from potential contractors. The contract having been awarded, the contracting organisation's plan usually becomes part of the contract and is the basis for progress reporting to the client organisation.

2. *The contracting organisation.* A contracting organisation specialises in implementing projects for client organisations. Generally, the opportunity to implement a client's project must be won in competition. Planning is required both as the basis of a proposal to the client and for the contracting organisation subsequently to implement the project. It does not matter what the project scope contains or what the technological solution might be: the contracting organisation needs a plan as the basis of its proposal to the client.

The plan must of course identify resources and costs and be the basis for the contractor to operate earned value type calculations if the project is of sufficient value and complexity. It must contain all the project objectives, particularly defined deliverables, to meet the required performance specification; and the plan, costed, underpins the price offered to the potential client. The resources required and defined in the schedule need to be available to complete the work, and the contracting organisation needs to ensure that, as a business, it has the resources available for the concurrent implementation of its portfolio of projects. This requires a resource management process to be in place built around the resource outputs from all of the organisation's project plans. This process also shows the times that the business has resource available, so the best use of resources can be made. Finally, prior to the final bid plan and price being submitted a risk review is held to ensure that some form of contingency or reserve is held against risks that might occur. This of course becomes the beginning of risk management for the contractor.

Once the contract has been awarded, monitoring and control needs to be performed, and the plan is the reference for measurement, of both time and cost. If the project is going well, then all is well, but if the plan starts to slip or the spend starts to exceed the budget on individual work packages, the variances against the plan identify the problem areas that need to be addressed by the project team to get the project back on track.

3. *The in-house projects organisation.* An in-house projects organisation itself requires the deliverables of the project, needs the benefits that the project is intended to deliver and pays for the project, choosing to implement the project itself. Planning is required to obtain the necessary approvals to proceed with the project, and subsequently to provide the baseline for project monitoring and control.

4
When to plan

Planning starts immediately the organisation identifies the probable need for a project, and continues throughout the project life cycle. The emphasis changes from strategic planning through detailed planning to monitoring and control using the plan, and while the project is being implemented action may be required to maintain the plan and to replan if necessary. Figure 4.1 illustrates the changing emphasis throughout the life cycle, and indicates typical timing of gate reviews – formal points in a project where its plan, progress, expected cost and benefits are reviewed and decisions are made on whether to continue to the next phase.

4.1 The concept phase

The concept phase is the first phase in the project life cycle. During this phase, the need, opportunity or problem is confirmed, the overall feasibility of the project is considered and a preferred solution is identified.

On behalf of the organisation, the project sponsor appoints the project manager and briefs him or her on the probable need for a project – *probable* at this stage because until the project has been defined it cannot be reviewed and approved for implementation. The nucleus of the project team is formed around the project manager and the concept phase begins.

Initially, there are mostly questions about the project and few answers – *there is, as yet, no plan*. The project manager should have a good idea of 'why' from the sponsor, and probably an indication of 'what', in terms of an outline of the objectives, scope and deliverables of the project. All the other planning questions must be answered. Planning is top-down and strategic, helping to develop the business case, and providing enough detail to justify continuing the project into the definition phase.

The concept phase is least expensive in terms of overall project effort, but planning is a large part of this effort. Moreover, effective planning is critical because it has maximum leverage on the likely success of the

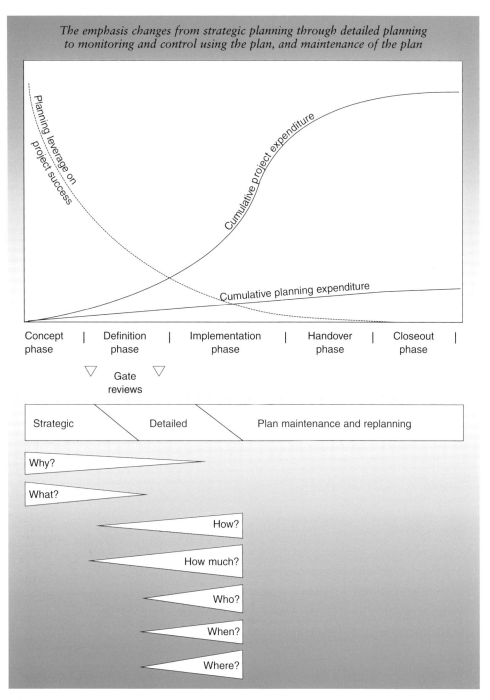

Figure 4.1 *Planning continues throughout the project life cycle*

project. Selection of the best implementation option and strategies is fundamental to effective implementation of the project.

The strategic plan is developed, with enough detail to inform the business case and a gate review at the end of the concept phase. If the sponsor and the organisation are convinced of the viability of the project, that it can deliver the desired benefits with acceptable risk to the organisation, it is allowed to continue into the definition phase.

4.2 The definition phase

During the definition phase the preferred solution is further evaluated and optimised – often an iterative process. This phase requires a transition from strategic to detailed planning, to work out the scope, time, cost and quality objectives of the project. The plan must be developed in sufficient detail to expose issues with the project to enable its implementation to be justified, and to provide a sound basis for implementation – a baseline against which the project subsequently can be monitored and controlled.

The questions 'why?' and 'what?' will have been answered in the concept phase – perhaps definitively, although there may be further refinements. Now, in the definition phase, 'how' is developed in more detail, enabling 'how much?', 'who?', 'when?' and 'where?' to be answered. The answers must be sufficiently robust:

- for client projects: to convince the sponsor, and via the sponsor the organisation, that the project may be proposed to the client, has a good chance of winning a contract from the client, and has a good chance of being successfully implemented;
- for internal projects: to convince the sponsor, and via the sponsor the organisation, that implementation of the project should be funded.

At the end of the definition phase, the plan should be baselined ready for use during implementation for monitoring and control purposes. Subsequent changes to the plan should be under formal change control.

4.3 The implementation phase

In the implementation phase, the plan is executed. The plan defines how the project should be implemented and provides the basis for monitoring and control. The project should be formally launched, at which time the plan is formally communicated to the project team and key stakeholders, including additional resources not involved in the concept and definition phases. Larger projects, particularly those applying earned value management, may hold an integrated baseline review (IBR) to confirm that the plan is correct and comprehensive and is agreed by the project team.

Planning activities in the implementation phase include:

- maintenance of the plan: definition and implementation of routine changes to the plan, under formal change control, to address minor variances;
- replanning: definition and implementation of changes to the plan, under formal change control, either within the existing scope (e.g. in response to critical variances) or with changes to scope (e.g. in response to client-requested changes).

On larger and longer-duration projects, organisations may operate rolling wave planning. Only the next stage of the implementation, or the next time window, is planned in enough detail for precise monitoring and control. The next stage/time window must be planned in greater detail and baselined prior to implementation.

4.4 The handover phase

During the handover phase, the project deliverables are handed over to the client and/or the users.

The plan defines how the project will be handed over to the client or to the internal users of the project's deliverables. Monitoring and control, plan maintenance and replanning continue as in the implementation phase.

Some projects have extended life cycles, including operation and disposal phases. In these phases, planning is again similar to the implementation phase.

4.5 The closeout phase

In the closeout phase, project matters are finalised, final project reviews are carried out, project information is archived and the project team is redeployed.

The valuable lessons learned at the end of a project should add to the organisation's knowledge bank to provide the building blocks for planning on future projects. Many of the lessons will be contained in the maintained plan – which at the end of the project will define exactly how implementation was carried out – and in reports arising from monitoring and control activities. The reports may contain information on variances and their causes: the causes can be identified as threats in future projects and planned out. Variances may require adjustments to organisational norms, so that better estimating data is available when future projects are planned, or to the organisation's processes.

5

Who plans?

Planning should engage all the key stakeholders in the project. It is led and co-ordinated by the project manager and undertaken by the project team. Planning cannot proceed effectively in isolation from any of the stakeholders – it must feed off the inputs from all informed parties.

5.1 The sponsor

The key role of the sponsor in project planning is to ensure that the project participants are focused on and committed to a common purpose and vision of success. The project manager can achieve this within the core project team, but it is the sponsor who can expand that commitment to include the wider organisation with its support functions.

Along with the management body that approves projects, the sponsor:

- sets the project priority
- provides funding
- approves resource levels
- approves the plan to enable the project manager to establish the baseline against which the project will be monitored and controlled.

In addition, the sponsor:

- considers the project interfaces that lie outside the control of the project manager;
- finalises (and approves any changes to) the project objectives and success criteria;
- ensures that the project team has the time and resources it needs to achieve success;
- communicates the project purpose and value to the organisation's senior management;

17

- commits specific resources from the organisation;
- paves the way for change in the affected organisational units;
- participates in major project reviews and approves key deliverables;
- makes or endorses strategic project decisions;
- ensures timely resolution of issues affecting project success.

5.2 The project manager

The project manager's role is to manage the planning process in order to deliver a good plan. The planning deliverables must be realised within the available budget and resources, and to a schedule that will satisfy the needs of project gate reviews and, where appropriate, deadlines for proposals to clients. The project manager is responsible for the deployment of effective planning processes by his or her team and for planning interfaces with key stakeholders. The project manager must keep the sponsor appraised of progress and as necessary escalate issues to the sponsor.

On smaller projects, the project manager may personally facilitate the planning process and capture the planning outputs; on larger projects, the project manager is likely to delegate the tasks to member(s) of the project team, which may include specialist planners.

5.3 The specialist planner

Planning, monitoring and control, risk management and change control are the basic processes of effective project management and are the responsibility of the project manager. In all but the smallest projects, the project manager is generally supported in the implementation of these processes by specialists planner(s). (Other titles such as scheduler and project co-ordinator may apply, depending on the organisation and the precise allocation of responsibilities.) In very large/complex projects, these 'specialist' roles may carry responsibility and accountability equal to that of managing the totality of a less complex project.

A planner is a specialist in project planning (and often in other project management processes) whose role is to facilitate the planning process in order to ensure that project's objectives are translated into an optimum plan. This is achieved by collating the inputs of the team and its subject matter expertise into the plan, requiring a proactive approach and good organisational, co-ordination, communication and problem-solving skills.

The planner should lead the project team's application of the software tools and techniques which are likely to be used to develop particular elements of the overall plan. In particular, the planner is likely to be the principal user of scheduling software, and will translate the project's WBS into schedule network logic and ultimately into the project schedule.

An experienced planner can bring invaluable experience of previous projects and the lessons learned from them, and hence can not only directly influence how the project will be implemented, but can help ensure its viability.

5.4 The WBS element owner/ control account manager

On larger projects, the project manager may delegate to other managers the responsibility for implementation of elements of the overall scope of work. These managers then 'own' and must deliver specific elements of the WBS. In organisations implementing earned value management, such managers are often termed control account managers (CAMs). The WBS element owner is accountable for ensuring that the defined scope of work for a particular WBS element (control account) is achieved to the budget, timescale and quality standards in accordance with the project requirements. WBS element owners are responsible for the development, execution and control of their work scope within the schedule. Each manages the WBS element as a contract with the project manager.

Delegation to WBS element owners should be based on their specific skills, experience and aptitude to manage the work. It follows that their involvement in the planning process ensures that their expertise improves the quality of the plan. In addition, involvement in the planning ensures that they achieve ownership of their scopes of work and are ready to hit the ground running when implementation starts.

The involvement of a WBS element owner in the planning process is a subset of the project manager's involvement. Each WBS element must be properly defined, scheduled and resourced – like a mini-project. But in addition, the WBS element must be integrated into the overall project, through consideration of internal dependencies and logical links to other WBS elements.

5.5 Other project team members and key stakeholders

The role of other project team members and stakeholders is to ensure that their specialist skills and experience contribute to the most effective plan. For example:

- System engineers should ensure that the plan includes the application of a rigorous system engineering process: design stages should be evident in the WBS and schedule and design reviews should be apparent as key milestones.
- Procurement specialists should ensure that the plan reflects an appropriate acquisition/procurement strategy, appropriate subcontract boundaries and realistic lead times.
- Manufacturing specialists should ensure that manufacturing set-up and low-rate initial production are included in the plan as required, and that production schedules and cost estimates are based on relevant norms for the organisation.
- Commercial specialists should satisfy themselves that the client's contractual requirements are met by the plan and contractual deliverables are aligned with the customer's required delivery schedule.

6

How to plan

6.1 Appropriateness

The *amount* of planning should be appropriate to the nature of the project. Considerations include:

- *Project size (cost) and complexity.* A high-cost project is not necessarily complex, but complexity does tend to increase with project size. Small projects may be complex, for example if including new technology or a complex supply chain. Large size/cost and complex projects typically require additional planning directly because of their size and complexity, and indirectly because the organisation requires a greater burden of proof of viability at gate reviews.
- *Project uncertainty and risk.* Uncertain or risky projects are likely to require additional planning, to reduce uncertainty and risk to levels acceptable to the organisation and to other key stakeholders.
- *Project criticality.* A project may be of high criticality to the organisation, for example a 'must win' contract or a key internal change project. Organisations are likely to require additional planning effort on such projects.
- *Time and resources available for planning.* Planning must be accomplished within constraints of available time and resources. Available time may be determined by a potential client's timescales for a response to a request for proposals; resources may be determined by the extent to which the project team can be formed prior to project launch and by the availability of specialist planners.

6.2 Planning techniques

The planning techniques used vary throughout the project life cycle, reflecting the transition from strategic to detailed planning and the evolving emphasis of the questions about the project that planning must

21

answer. Not all of these techniques are planning-specific – many have other project management applications, and some are wider than project management – but they can all contribute to effective planning. Figure 6.1 shows the relationship of some of the techniques to strategic and detailed planning; Appendix B briefly defines these and other techniques.

Planning techniques need to be chosen carefully. The aim is to assist the project manager and the team, and through them the sponsor and the key stakeholders, to conceptualise and define the project, and to provide the baseline for monitoring and control. The techniques used should be relevant, appropriate and cost-effective. They need to be neither so simple that they ignore significant issues, nor so complex as to confuse matters. The project manager's experience in project planning, often aided by that of the specialist planner(s), determines the techniques appropriate to the project.

6.3 Strategic planning

Planning in the early phases of the project life cycle is strategic rather than detailed: it is top-down and focuses on 'why', 'what' and 'how'. The answers to these questions provide the strategic framework for the project plan. The project manager asks 'why' and 'how' questions of the project sponsor and other key stakeholders in structured interviews. The client is a key stakeholder but may not be directly accessible to the project manager, in a situation where the organisation is participating in competitive bidding for a contract to undertake the client's project. In this situation, indirect means may need to be employed to obtain the client's perspective: informal contacts, stakeholder analysis and market intelligence. Some of the answers given will prompt further research or analysis. Requirements management may commence.

For an internal project for the organisation, the answer to 'why?' is often in the form of a business objective, to move an organisation from its present position to a desired future state. The vehicle that delivers this change is a project, and planning provides the route. It therefore follows that the answer to 'why?' may be found in the business plan.

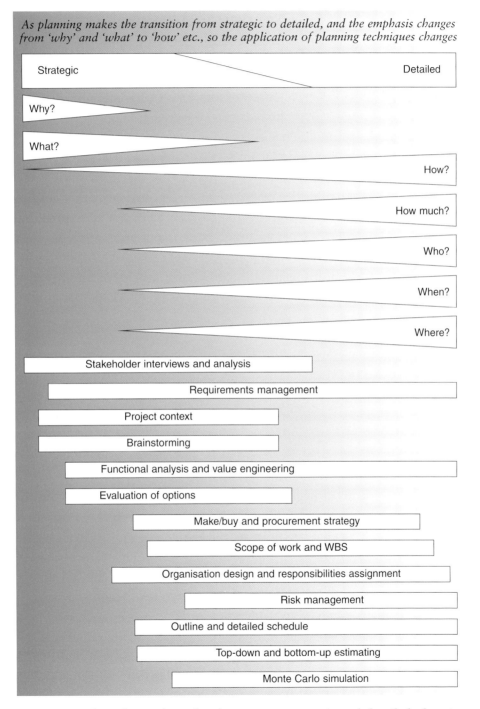

Figure 6.1 *The relationship of techniques to strategic and detailed planning*

Of course a client's or an organisation's objective could be satisfied in a number of different ways. In response to the question 'what?', the answer may be a physical structure, an organisational change or a new procedure, and is frequently found to be a combination of these elements. It is likely to require the systematic evaluation of alternatives, including trade studies, and is likely to be closely linked with conceptual design of the technical solution. For a complex project, significant time and effort are likely to be expended in answering 'what?'.

While the sponsor and/or the client principally determine 'why' and 'what', the answer to 'how?' is principally the responsibility of the project team. Answering how the project is to be delivered should call on all the expertise that the project team and the wider organisation can muster. A review of lessons learned on similar projects can provide valuable suggestions and help avoid previous pitfalls. Answering 'how?' requires effective communication within the project team and with functional experts elsewhere in the organisation.

Strategic planning must provide preliminary answers to the other planning questions – at a level of detail consistent with the formulation of the strategic plan and sufficient to pass gate reviews. 'How much?' addresses the resources required, and in strategic planning is likely to be answered by top-down estimating using comparative or parametric techniques to produce an order of magnitude or rough order of magnitude (ROM) cost. The answer to 'how much?' is of particular importance to the investment appraisal usually required in the business case.

'Who' is addressed at organisation level and is likely to involve consideration of the core competencies and capacity, driving the organisation's acquisition/procurement, outsourcing and manufacturing strategies. The extent to which the project is implemented in house will be determined: whether the organisation will seek risk-sharing partners (perhaps to access particular competencies or capacities of the partners), what will be sub-contracted and the extent to which commodity procurements will be involved. For an overseas client, there may be offset requirements to be addressed. Considerations of offset and outsourcing touch on 'where?'

An outline schedule is developed to address 'when'. The organisation must determine whether the project is likely to satisfy its own or the client's implementation timescales. Large and complex projects may justify the use of probabilistic techniques (Monte Carlo simulation) to evaluate the range of probable outcomes for the project.

Strategic planning should consider the context of the project – the political, economic, social, technological and legal environment in which it will be implemented – and this is likely to help define factors critical to the project's success.

The strategic planning process which deploys the strategic planning techniques is summarised in Figure 6.2. Strategic planning is highly creative and, like many creative activities, is highly iterative: Figure 6.2 gives only an impression of the steps likely to be involved in strategic planning for anything other than the simplest projects.

The outputs of strategic planning are captured in an initial version of the PMP. Some outputs will populate other documents, such as the business plan, and all will be drawn on at gate reviews – particularly the one at the end of the concept phase, which seeks authorisation to proceed with the project definition phase.

6.4 Detailed planning

Detailed planning should commence only when the strategic plan for the project is sufficiently mature. False starts may be made, and scarce time and resources wasted, if detailed planning commences using the wrong implementation strategy or the wrong technical solution. The sponsor and the key stakeholders should endorse the strategic plan and particularly the 'what' and the 'how' before detailed planning commences – though planning is usually highly iterative and detailed planning should be allowed to refine 'what' and 'how' and in extreme cases may even challenge 'why', prompting a review of the overall rationale for the project.

'How' is developed by defining the scope of work, using a WBS. The WBS should closely reflect the processes that the organisation will use to implement the project, both to ensure completeness of the scope of work and also to ensure that the plan is naturally and instinctively followed by those performing the work. Each element of the WBS can be defined and documented (for example in a WBS dictionary) and detailed statements of work (SoWs) can be prepared for subcontracts.

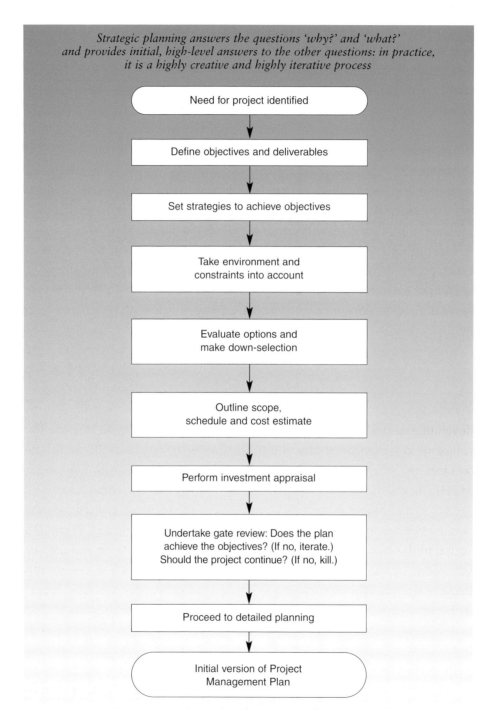

Figure 6.2 *The strategic planning process*

'How much' and 'who' develop with the scope of work: an organisation best suited to implement the scope of work is designed alongside the WBS and defined in an organisation breakdown structure. The resulting responsibility assignment matrix, mapping the work to the organisation, should demonstrate straightforward mapping so that there is no ambiguity when implementation commences. Organisational resources are assigned to activities to help develop the detailed, bottom-up cost estimate that will be the basis of the project's budget. Consideration of where the work will be undertaken will inform decisions about needs for new facilities, transportation, export licensing and communications. Identification, analysis and evaluation of risks will enable measures to avoid threats and exploit opportunities to be built into the plan, and will determinate how much contingency provision should be allowed for threats which cannot be eliminated.

'When' involves development of a detailed schedule for the project or, for a larger project, a set of schedules usually consisting of a project master schedule and subordinate, detailed schedules. Scheduling involves capturing the activities of the WBS in the time domain, usually using scheduling software and most frequently presented as a Gantt chart. Definition of the relationships between the activities – the network logic – and of the duration of the activities enables the schedule to be developed. External constraints and dependencies must be addressed. The timing of key milestones can then be determined, and if they are found not to meet the project's requirements, the project's critical path can be re-examined and revised until the project's timing is satisfactory.

Detailed planning generates copious amounts of data, and it is important to ensure that the project team is not swamped by it. The data is sorted and quantified into appropriate groups for the purpose of building the plan. Hierarchical coding structures can be used to assist in this process, and product, work, organisation, resource, cost and risk breakdown structures may all be applicable. The sponsor and key stakeholders cannot be expected to review all of the detailed planning information but must achieve confidence in it by the presentation of suitable summaries such as high-level schedules, 'top 10' risks and cost/budget summaries.

The detailed planning process which deploys the detailed planning techniques is summarised in Figure 6.3. Detailed planning is still creative but is more structured than strategic planning, using more 'hard' techniques

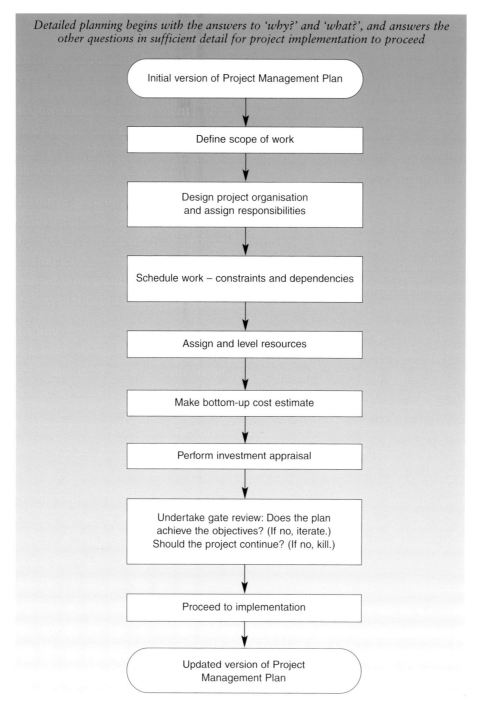

Figure 6.3 *The detailed planning process*

and usually needing specialist software tools. Iteration is required to refine and optimise the detailed plan.

The outputs of detailed planning are captured in an updated version of the PMP. Some outputs will populate other documents, such as an updated business plan, and all will be drawn on at gate reviews – particularly the one at the end of the definition phase, which seeks authorisation to proceed with project implementation. Where the project is the subject of a proposal to a client, the detailed planning provides much of the information required to form the proposal.

7

Characteristics of good planning

Good planning delivers a plan that defines the implementation of the project that is mostly likely to ensure achievement of the project's objectives. The plan must be realistic and achievable, and must:

- be owned by the project manager and the project team;
- be agreed by the sponsor, on behalf of the organisation, and by other key stakeholders;
- sufficiently answer the planning questions to satisfy the organisation, via gate reviews, that it should continue the project;
- in competition for a client-funded project, provide the basis for a winning proposal;
- provide the basis for effective management of project implementation, and for effective monitoring and control of the project.

Good planning harnesses all the skills and experience of the project manager and his or her project team, and of the wider organisation and the lessons it has learned. It must also reflect the views and inputs of the key stakeholders. Good planning must also deliver the plan on time: the best plan, if just too late, is useless. In short, planning has dimensions of scope, time, cost and quality – it is a mini-project in its own right, requiring the skills of the project manager to perform it.

Ultimately, even the best planning cannot guarantee project success. Events foreseen as risks do occur, and events which could not have been predicted during the project concept and definition phases may occur which can hinder the achievement of project objectives. The project manager must then rely on other attributes of effective project management to bring the project to a successful conclusion. But while no guarantee of success, good project planning is one of the best ways of avoiding project failure.

APPENDIX A
Further information

Relationship to APM Body of Knowledge

This APM *Introduction to Project Planning* develops and expands on principles described in the *APM Body of Knowledge*, 5th edition, in the following sections in particular:

2 Planning the Strategy
    2.2 Stakeholder Management
    2.6 Project Quality Management
3 Executing the Strategy
    3.1 Scope Management
    3.2 Scheduling
    3.3 Resource Management
    3.4 Budgeting and Cost Management
    3.6 Earned Value Management

Further reading

The above sections of the *APM Body of Knowledge* include reading lists identifying documents containing additional information on project planning.

Terminology

Terminology used in this booklet is generally consistent with the Glossary of Project Management Terms contained in the *APM Body of Knowledge*.

Website

Association for Project Management: www.apm.org.uk

Abbreviations and acronyms

APM	Association for Project Management
APM BoK	Body of Knowledge
CAM	Control account manager
DCF	Discounted cash flow
IBR	Integrated baseline review
IRR	Internal rate of return
NPV	Net present value
OBS	Organisation breakdown structure
PERT	Programme evaluation and review technique
PMP	Project management plan
RAM	Responsibility assignment matrix
ROM	Rough order of magnitude
SIG	Specific Interest Group
SoW	Statement of work
WBS	Work breakdown structure

APPENDIX B
Planning techniques

Not all of these techniques are planning-specific – many have other project management applications and some are wider than project management – but they can all contribute to effective planning.

ADePT A technique for planning and controlling design and engineering projects which accounts for the iterative nature of design/engineering, while planning the information flow through such projects and identifying key design decisions.

Benchmarking The review of what other organisations are doing in the same area. Organisations that appear to be particularly successful in what they do and how they do it may be taken as examples to be emulated, i.e. used as benchmarks.

Bottom-up estimating An estimating technique based on making estimates for every work package (or activity) in the work breakdown structure and summarising them to provide an overall estimate of the effort and cost required.

Brainstorming The unstructured generation of ideas by a group of people in a short space of time.

Budget estimate An approximate estimate prepared in the early phases of a project to establish financial viability or to secure resources.

Budgeting and cost management The estimating of costs and the setting of an agreed budget; the management of actual and forecast costs against the budget.

Cash flow forecast A prediction of the difference between cash received and payments made during a specific period for the duration of a project.

Communication The giving, receiving, processing and interpretation of information. Information can be conveyed verbally, non-verbally, actively, passively, formally, informally, consciously and unconsciously.

Comparative estimating An estimating technique based on the comparison with, and factoring from, the cost of a previous similar project or operation.

Cost–benefit analysis An analysis of the relationship between the costs of undertaking an activity or project, initial and recurrent, and the benefits likely to arise from the changed situation, initially and recurrently.

Cost estimating The process of predicting the costs of a project.

Critical chain A networking technique based on Goldratt's theory of constraints that identifies paths through a project based on resource dependencies, as well as technological precedence requirements.

Critical path analysis The procedure for calculating the critical path and floats in a network/schedule.

Critical path method A technique used to predict project duration by analysing which sequence of activities has the least amount of scheduling flexibility.

Delphi technique A process where a consensus view is reached by consultation with experts. It is often used as an estimating technique.

Discounted cash flow (DCF) The concept of relating future cash inflows and outflows over the life of a project or operation to a common base value, thereby allowing more validity in the comparison of different projects with different durations and rates of cash flow.

Estimating The use of a range of techniques and tools to produce estimates.

Force field analysis A technique used to identify the various pressures promoting or resisting change.

Functional analysis The identification and analysis of the functional attributes of different solutions.

Impact analysis An assessment of the effect on project objectives of a proposed change or of a risk occurring.

Integrated baseline review (IBR) A review following the establishment of the initial baseline, to ensure that it is comprehensive and correct and understood by the organisation.

Investment appraisal The appraisal of the value of a project, involving cash flow forecasting, discounted cash flow analysis and the calculation of payback period and internal rate of return.

Issue log A log of all the issues raised during the planning or execution of a project; during planning, it helps ensure that issues are resolved prior to implementation.

Last planner A technique for identifying short-term 'look ahead' schedules based on a master schedule, and analysing constraints on activities which may prevent them being completed in accordance with the master schedule. The technique includes robust measures of progress of the rate at which activities in the schedule are completed.

Make-or-buy decision The decision to make a deliverable internally or to buy it from a supplier: for example, whether to develop a software application in house or to purchase an existing or bespoke software application.

Monte Carlo simulation A technique used to estimate the likely range of outcomes from a complex process or project, by simulating the process under randomly selected conditions a large number of times.

Network analysis A method used to calculate a project's critical path and activity times and float.

Order of magnitude/rough order of magnitude (ROM) estimate An estimate carried out to give a very approximate indication of expected cost.

Organisation design The design of the most appropriate organisation for a project.

Parametric estimating An estimating technique that uses a statistical relationship between historical data and other variables (for example square metreage in construction, lines of code in software development) to calculate an estimate.

Pareto technique A technique to identify the minority of variables with the greatest impact on project objectives (familiar as the '20:80 rule').

Product flow diagram A diagram representing how products are produced by identifying their derivation and the relationships between them. It is similar to a network diagram, but includes products rather than activities.

Programme evaluation and review technique (PERT) A technique for determining how much time a project needs to complete.

Quality planning The process of determining which quality standards are applicable and how to apply them.

Requirements management The process of capturing, analysing and testing the stated needs of a client/user/stakeholder.

Resource planning The process of identifying, assigning and levelling the resources needed by a project to enable the project to be implemented with available resources in an acceptable duration.

Rolling wave planning An approach to planning in which only the current phase or time period of a project is planned in detail, future phases being planned in outline only. Each phase produces a detailed plan for the next phase.

Scheduling The process used to determine the sequence of activities in a project and its overall duration. This includes determining the logical interdependencies between activities and estimating activity durations, taking into account requirements and available resources.

Sensitivity analysis An investigation of the effect on the outcome of changing parameters or data.

Simulation A process whereby some dynamic aspect of a system or project is replicated (modelled) without using the real system, often using computerised techniques.

Stakeholder analysis The identification of stakeholders, their interest levels and their ability to influence a project.

Three-point estimate An estimate in which an optimistic value (quickest, cheapest), a most likely value and a pessimistic value (slowest, most expensive) are all defined.

Top-down cost estimating An estimate of project cost based on historical costs and other project variables, subdivided down to individual work packages or activities.

Value engineering Optimisation of the conceptual, technical and operational aspects of a project's deliverables.

APPENDIX C

Information about the APM Planning SIG

Membership and mission

The APM Planning Specific Interest Group (SIG), reformed during 2007, comprises representatives of the aerospace and defence, construction, nuclear and rail sectors, as well as cross-sector project managers. The members of the SIG believe that good project planning is critical to project success and should therefore be at the heart of the project management process. Accordingly the Planning SIG should be considered as a link between existing APM SIGs.

The Planning SIG's mission is to advance and raise the profile and professionalism of project planning by:

- documenting and disseminating best practice
- instigating debate in the APM and elsewhere on planning practice
- advancing the state of the art
- enhancing educational frameworks for planning
- reinforcing the professionalism and enhancing the standing of planners
- contributing to future issues of the *APM Body of Knowledge*.

Next steps

The Planning SIG is keen to receive feedback from the project planning community on this APM *Introduction to Project Planning*. Our contact details are listed over the page.

Why join the planning SIG?

Membership of the APM Planning SIG is open to all APM members and to representatives of corporate members who have a particular interest in project planning.

As a member of the APM Planning SIG, you will be able to:

- be part of the leading UK group addressing project planning matters;
- share views and concerns and exchange information with other planning professionals;
- participate in the development of best practice, guidance, standards and educational frameworks for project planning;
- help to foster relationships with business and with other professional groups.

How to contact us

For further information about the Planning SIG, or to provide feedback on this document, please e-mail us at planningsig@apm.org.uk.